Blessed Assurance

31 DEVOTIONAL INSIGHTS *based on the hymns of* FANNY CROSBY

LUCAS & HANNAH SHROUT

Shrout
Music Ministry

Blessed Assurance: 31 Devotional Insights Based on the Hymns of Fanny Crosby

Copyright © 2013 by Shrout Music Ministry, PO Box 970, Penns Creek, PA 17862

ISBN 978-1-62620-251-1

Cover image © by Pedro Tavares.
Design by Jon Plank
Printed in the United States of America

A biography of
FRANCES JANE (FANNY) CROSBY
by NATHAN PURDY

Fanny Jane Crosby was born in Southeast, New York, on March 24, 1820. To many, it might seem as though her life got off on the wrong note. If they were to choose a soundtrack for the first year of her life, it would not be a soft, soothing lullaby. Instead, they would find the slow, sad lament of a mournful dirge more fitting. Before Fanny reached her first birthday, the funeral chimes rang out for her father, John. However, his untimely death wasn't the only loss the family grieved that year. While Mercy, her mother, stood by the grave, she was still reeling from the discovery that Fanny was blind – the frustrating result of a quack's faulty prescription when Fanny was only six weeks old. Despite her mother's tireless efforts, including a visit to the famed Dr. Mott in New York City, no remedy could be found. Dr. Mott's words, "Poor child, I am afraid you will never see again,"[1] brought the familiar sound of a death knell – this time to Mercy's fading hopes. For her life, until she died in Bridgeport, Connecticut, on February 12, 1915, aged ninety-four, Fanny's eyes would never see a bird soar, a flower bloom, a face smile, or a sun rise.

Some might complain that the hand of fate had dealt Fanny a cruel draw. They might say that she was unlucky - a victim. But such thoughts, if they dared tip-toe into her mind, were in for a shocking reception. For God was working things out. In particular, he allowed Fanny to spend time with two godly ladies. As a result of her father's passing, Mercy had to work to make ends meet. Consequently, Fanny spent long hours with her grandmother, Eunice, "a woman of exemplary piety." They would sit together in their favorite rocking chair, and Fanny would soak up the godly, gentle instruction. Then they would kneel in prayer beside that old rocking chair and talk to God, with a simple confidence that He would hear and answer. Moreover, when her family relocated to Ridgefield, Connecticut, they lived with a Mrs. Hawley, a pious lady whose love of poetry and passion for Scripture memorization rubbed off on Fanny – even as a child, she had memorized the Penta-teuch, the Gospels, Proverbs, and the Song of Solomon. So, when thoughts of 'blind chance' wandered into her mind, they were immediately felled by a volley of Scripture verses and her grandmother's kind instruction.

When only eight or nine years old, Fanny wrote:

Oh, what a happy soul I am, / Although I cannot see!
I am resolved that in this world / Contented I will be.
How many blessings I enjoy / That other people don't,
To weep and sigh because I'm blind / I cannot, and I won't!

This poetic expression of deep feeling provides a tantalizing example of what was to come. And it illustrates just how incredi-ble God's grace is. Evidently, God had given Fanny an epic talent to turn a phrase. He took those seemingly tragic events of her infancy, gave her grace to embrace them, and used them to guide her feet to a path that otherwise she might never have found. In 1834, in a direct answer to prayer, He opened the door for her to attend the recently opened New York Institute for the Blind, where she received a helpful education. In 1850, He brought her into a place of real spiritual clarity, when she prayed through at a revival altar, and jumped to her feet with shouts of "Hallelujah!" He allowed her path to cross with such giants of hymnody as George Root and William Bradbury. God was working to prepare her for her life's calling. This is ex-actly how Fanny came to see it. Referring to the trickster whose foolish advice blinded her, she would later write, "I have not for a moment in more than eighty-five years, felt a spark of resentment against him because I have always believed from my youth to this very moment that the good Lord, in His infinite mercy, by this means consecrated me to the work that I am still permitted to do."

The 'work' that Fanny was called to do had many parts. She had influence as a teacher in the Institute for the Blind. Her calling included becoming a wife to Alexander van Alistine in 1858. After leaving the Institute, Fanny launched into an influential ministry of speaking to thousands in revivals and wielding influence in Sunday Schools. She was personally ac-quainted with presidents and people of power. However, her particular 'work' was, of course, penning over 8,000 hymns. These masterpieces of sincere devotion are so true and honest to Christian feeling that millions have found them a word-per-fect expression of their own hearts' aspirations. Choirs have found their hearts soaring in heavenly places as they have sung

"Praise Him!" Soloists hearts have melted in worship as they sung "Blessed Assurance, Jesus is Mine." Congregations have found their marching orders to Christian service in "Rescue the Perishing." Residents in nursing homes have hummed "All the Way My Savior Leads Me" in their darkest hour of lonely fear, and found it a reassuring arm around their shoulders.

Without a doubt, Fanny could have lived her life in a minor key. Victim. Disadvantaged. Bitter. Blind. But she chose not to. This, of course, baffled many, who wished they could rewind her life and change the key of that first year. However, Fanny had come to the powerful realization that we cannot fully appreciate the major keys without the minors – and God can bring them all together to compose a tune that will bless, enrich, and edify millions. It's why she could say, "Do you know that if at birth I had been able to make one petition, it would have been that I was born blind?" Why? "Because when I get to heaven, the first face that shall ever gladden my sight will be that of my Savior." Why be a victim, when there is grace sufficient to make you a victor?

[1] Fanny J. Crosby, *Fanny J. Crosby: An Autobiography*, (Peabody, Massachusetts: Hendrickson Publishers, 2008), 22.

Pass Me Not

AND THE PUBLICAN, STANDING AFAR OFF, WOULD NOT LIFT UP SO MUCH AS HIS EYES UNTO
HEAVEN, BUT SMOTE UPON HIS BREAST, SAYING, GOD BE MERCIFUL TO ME A SINNER.
LUKE 18:13

Day 1

In the stillness of the moment, when the Spirit is speaking, we find ourselves thinking… praying…. Our hearts are warmed as we ponder the gentle Savior calling the lost to Himself. We recall the time when condemnation and guilt was the steady staple of life, and fear and disappointment was more common than not.

> HE IS NOT
> CONFUSED
> ABOUT MY
> SITUATION….

The call of Christ came when we could do nothing to save ourselves, when the weight of who we really were was far more burdensome to bear than to live, and deep grief over what we had done was overwhelming to the mind and spirit. How could He call out in love despite what we had been?

It matters not where we find ourselves when the Savior calls; we only have to listen. Right now, whatever the need that arises in your life—He is able to touch you where you are. Don't go on toting more than you can humanly bear. As He calls, give your burdens to Him—He will not pass you by.

Pass me not, O gentle Savior;
Hear my humble cry.
While on others Thou art calling,
Do not pass me by.

Let me at the throne of mercy,
Find a sweet relief;
Kneeling there in deep contrition,
Help my unbelief.

Savior, Savior,
Hear my humble cry.
While on others Thou art calling,
Do not pass me by.

7

Searching, seeking Savior,

Let Your gaze find me (even) today. I need Your peace, mercy, and love. There is nothing good in me, save You and what You have done.

My mind runs so quickly and my duties seem so endless. It is not easy to be quiet before You. The chaos of this world confuses and alarms me. To know that You see and hear me, what joy! To know that You love, what rest!

Shepherd of lost sheep,

My heart longs to know You. In Your mercy, seek my soul today. With Your will, guide my steps.

Do not pass me by.

8

Pass Me Not

BUT HE WAS WOUNDED FOR OUR TRANSGRESSIONS, HE WAS BRUISED
FOR OUR INIQUITIES: THE CHASTISEMENT OF OUR PEACE WAS UPON HIM;
AND WITH HIS STRIPES WE ARE HEALED. ISAIAH 53:5

I think of my father's testimony, how he knelt in a small country Baptist church to find his sins forgiven. Knowing little about the Gospel story, all he could picture in his mind was the bleeding Christ on the cross calling out to him.

His testimony is true for all of us – we come to Him in full understanding that we have blown it big time and that we are at the full mercy of God. He knows that we are broken, helpless, and dying, so He comes to heal, restore, and give life. Time and time again He brings us to the point where we realize that all we need is – Him.

> **WE COME TO HIM IN FULL UNDERSTANDING THAT WE HAVE BLOWN IT BIG TIME AND THAT WE ARE AT THE FULL MERCY OF GOD.**

Desperate for Life? – He gives Freedom
Desperate for Acceptance? – He gives Love
Desperate for Mercy? – He gives Grace.
Desperate for Hope? – He gives a Clean Heart
Desperate for Forgiveness? – He gives Eternal Life
Desperate for Peace? – He gives Healing
Desperate for Change? – He gives a New Beginning

Emmanuel,
Your name means, God with us. You came to know us personally. You took our place and redeemed us to Yourself. Thank You for life everlasting.

Trusting only in Thy merit,
Would I seek Thy face,
Heal my wounded, broken spirit.
Save me by thy grace.

Thou, the Spring of all my comfort,
More than life to me,
Whom have I on earth beside Thee?
Whom in heav'n but Thee?

Savior, Savior,
Hear my humble cry,
While on others Thou art calling,
Do not pass me by.

9

Day 3

All The Way My Savior Leads Me

THE LORD IS MY SHEPHERD; I SHALL NOT WANT. HE MAKETH ME TO LIE DOWN IN GREEN PASTURES: HE LEADETH ME BESIDE THE STILL WATERS. HE RESTORETH MY SOUL: HE LEADETH ME IN THE PATHS OF RIGHTEOUSNESS FOR HIS NAME'S SAKE. YEA, THOUGH I WALK THROUGH THE VALLEY OF THE SHADOW OF DEATH, I WILL FEAR NO EVIL: FOR THOU ART WITH ME; THY ROD AND THY STAFF THEY COMFORT ME. THOU PREPAREST A TABLE BEFORE ME IN THE PRESENCE OF MINE ENEMIES: THOU ANOINTEST MY HEAD WITH OIL; MY CUP RUNNETH OVER. SURELY GOODNESS AND MERCY SHALL FOLLOW ME ALL THE DAYS OF MY LIFE: AND I WILL DWELL IN THE HOUSE OF THE LORD FOR EVER. PSALM 23

All the way my Savior leads me;
What have I to ask beside?
Can I doubt His tender mercy,
Who through life has been my Guide?
Heav'nly peace, divinest comfort,
Here by faith in Him to dwell!
For I know, whate'er befall me,
Jesus doeth all things well;
For I know, whate'er befall me,
Jesus doeth all things well.

Sometimes I find myself so distracted with what I want to become or where I might want to go that I fail to see where Christ is leading me at the present moment. Afraid of being labeled a loser, being distraught at the possibility of failure, or consistently dwelling upon a past failure can so consume me that it is nearly impossible for "heavenly peace" or "divine comfort" to penetrate my soul. These are moments when I have let doubt obscure the way of faith. In these moments I begin to ask questions of my own personal self-worth, my own self-gain, and a host of other conflicts that He never intended for me to experience. The realization dawns upon me that I have been trying to take the lead on the pathway of life instead of trusting Him.

HE IS NOT CONFUSED ABOUT MY SITUATION....

To take my hands off and allow God to have complete control of life often leaves me feeling vulnerable. Fear of my world becoming too complex and anxiety over future plans and ambitions all beckon me to "doubt His tender mercy." It is in the every day decisions and grind of life that I must have enough faith to live outside my own expectations and let the Spirit do His work in and through me.

10

So I will rest in Him today, He already knows the path ahead. He is not confused about my situation, and I can allow my faith to be firmly anchored in the fact: "Jesus doeth all things well."

A weary soul I am today
   Tired of seeking my own way
Lead me gently in Thy pastures
   I will trust Thy guiding hand.

How can I pretend to know, Lord
   All the richness of Your plan
Take my life, dear Lord, I give it
   To thy love and care alone

There is rest when You are leading
   What a peace to trust in Thee.
Take my troubles, Lord, and use them
   As a means to strengthen me

Though the way I can't see clearly
   You the way before have trod
I will follow where You lead me
   For You lead me straight to God

Day 4

All the way my Savior leads me,
  Cheers each winding path I tread;
Gives me grace for every trial,
  Feeds me with the living Bread.
Though my weary steps may falter,
  And my soul athirst may be,
Gushing from the Rock before me,
  Lo! A spring of joy I see;
Gushing from the Rock before me,
  Lo! A spring of joy I see.

12

All The Way My Savior Leads Me

THEN HE SAID UNTO THEM, GO YOUR WAY, EAT THE FAT, AND DRINK THE SWEET, AND SEND PORTIONS UNTO THEM FOR WHOM NOTHING IS PREPARED: FOR THIS DAY IS HOLY UNTO OUR LORD: NEITHER BE YE SORRY; FOR THE JOY OF THE LORD IS YOUR STRENGTH. NEHEMIAH 8:10

The "gushing spring of joy" in this stanza takes us back to the Old Testament when God supplied water from a rock for the people of Israel. I can only imagine the thrill the children of Israel felt as they saw a dry solid rock become a refreshing, vibrant spring. Hot, tired, and thirsty even to the point of death, they celebrated as the need of water was supplied for a whole nation!

Sitting in a Bible College class room one morning, several classmates and I were bellyaching about busy schedules, hectic work loads, traveling appointments, and at the top of the list—utter exhaustion. The complaints went on for several minutes until finally our English professor looked out over her desk and said with authority, "Have any of you in this room heard of the joy of the Lord being your strength?" As you can imagine, it got deathly quiet as we freshmen ducked our heads in embarrassment at the very pointed question.

A preacher friend of mine once said, "I'm sure that many Christians run with their dipstick of joy pretty low." I have to agree. Thirsty, weary, and nearly to the point of spiritual defeat, we grumble about our circumstances, about the church, about work, about the children, about life! I think we need to get our sights off of our circumstances and set them on the gushing spring of joy.

I'm trying to make it a practice to see the gushing spring of joy that is available for all God's children. The key is in taking the time needed to allow the Spirit to do His work in us every day. So, we study His Word, we read devotion-

GUSHING FROM THE ROCK BEFORE ME, LO! A SPRING OF JOY I SEE.

als, we sing hymns and spiritual songs, and by these actions in and through prayer we make ourselves available to the joy of the Lord. Ask Christ to allow you a glimpse into the fullness of His joy and then drink deeply.

Jesus, the woman at the well came thirsty to You. You gave her water that she would never thirst again. Living Water.

Joy is like that water – a limitless supply. You promised Your joy would be our strength. Thank You for a bubbling stream that flows no matter what the circumstances. Today, let me have yet another thirst–quenching drink from Your gushing stream of joy.

All The Way My Savior Leads Me

I GO TO PREPARE A PLACE FOR YOU. AND IF I GO AND PREPARE A PLACE FOR YOU, I WILL COME AGAIN, AND RECEIVE YOU UNTO MYSELF: THAT WHERE I AM, THERE YE MAY BE ALSO.
JOHN 14:2-3

As a child and a young man, I heard more about heaven than what I'm hearing these days. Coming from a conservative church in the south, things could get quite lively in the sanctuary when there was singing or preaching about heaven. I'm not sure if the church family has become more cultured or too attached to earthly goods. Whatever the case, it would seem there isn't as much focus on "the land that is fairer than day." At any rate, I miss the feeling of honest anticipation and uninhibited joy often felt in those worship services.

Jesus' promise to be with us always, even until the end of the age, is still the consolation of every Christian. No matter how comfortable we become with this life, there is an undeniable anxiety for any of us to face the path we all must take. Yet, the child of God who has been led by the hand of the Savior will still find Him there at the end of the way. The stark reality of death is overcome by the victory of eternal life, the presence of Jesus, and the reunion of family and friends. The celebration will dissipate any memory of this old world and our song will be through the endless ages—Jesus led me all the way.

A TALK WITH GOD...

"Here Mommy, I draw a picture of you!"

Those early portraits are so abstract…just a roundish circle with some eyes. As my children grow, their perceptions change; their portraits have legs, arms, and even clothes!

As You lead me, Lord, I see Your kingdom more clearly. I see the rest You promise in Your presence. I see that someday I will understand in full Your promises. You will lead me to the place that is more real, more alive than I can imagine. Heaven – Jesus lead me all the way!

All the way my Savior leads me
O the fullness of His love!
Perfect rest to me is promised
In my Father's house above.
When my spirit, clothed immortal,
Wings its flight to realms of day
This my song through endless ages—
Jesus led me all the way;
This my song through endless ages—
Jesus led me all the way.

15

Day 6

Blessed assurance, Jesus is mine!
O what a foretaste of glory divine!
Heir of salvation, purchase of God,
Born of His Spirit, washed in His blood.

This is my story, this is my song,
Praising my Savior, all the day long;
This is my story, this is my song,
Praising my Savior, all the day long.

SOME QUESTIONS TO ASK YOURSELF:

- Can my co-workers see Jesus in me?
- Does my heart still rejoice at my new birth?
- Will I testify in some manner today with my faith?
- Are my actions speaking louder than my words as a Child of God?

Blessed Assurance

JESUS ANSWERED AND SAID UNTO HIM, VERILY, VERILY, I SAY UNTO THEE, EXCEPT A MAN BE BORN AGAIN, HE CANNOT SEE THE KINGDOM OF GOD. NICODEMUS SAITH UNTO HIM, HOW CAN A MAN BE BORN WHEN HE IS OLD? CAN HE ENTER THE SECOND TIME INTO HIS MOTHER'S WOMB, AND BE BORN? JESUS ANSWERED, VERILY, VERILY, I SAY UNTO THEE, EXCEPT A MAN BE BORN OF WATER AND OF THE SPIRIT, HE CANNOT ENTER INTO THE KINGDOM OF GOD. THAT WHICH IS BORN OF THE FLESH IS FLESH; AND THAT WHICH IS BORN OF THE SPIRIT IS SPIRIT. MARVEL NOT THAT I SAID UNTO THEE, YE MUST BE BORN AGAIN. JOHN 3:3-7

The third chapter of John gives a glimpse into a conversation between a curious, sincere religious leader and the Son of God. Little did Nicodemus know that his curiosity would generate a discussion that would become by far one of the most common and powerful means of communicating the gospel message. "Ye must be born again" are the words from Jesus to Nicodemus. The rabbi is confused by such a dramatic description. Jesus unfolds for Nicodemus the plan of salvation. He gently tries to lift the veil of spiritual darkness from the eyes of one who knew the Sacred Scrolls so well.

Men are still baffled at the words of Jesus. Until their eyes can be trained by the spirit of Christ to understand the Scriptures, they mock the church and its ways. However, scoffers find it hard to ignore the genuine testimony of a child of God. The life truly transformed or "born again", as Jesus said to Nicodemus, lives out its testimony as a new man or woman.

It is hard to comprehend that any of us can become the child of God. To realize that we indeed become the recipients of the eternal life promised to those who believe is overwhelming! It's not so important that we understand the mysteries of the new birth as it is to experience the forgiveness of sins.

Jesus, friend of sinners, what a joy to call You mine! You call me Your child, bought with Your blood. Let me not forget the price that has been paid. May my life sing the story so all may know You!

> SCOFFERS FIND IT HARD TO IGNORE THE GENUINE TESTIMONY OF A CHILD OF GOD.

16

Blessed Assurance

Day 7

CD Track: 3

The necessity of submission is often a difficult lesson to apprehend. As parents, we try to mold the will of a child, for his own safety and well being, to be submissive to authority. It's not always easy as the way is trodden with heart to heart talks, times of weighty discipline, and lots of tears and love. Our relationship to the Heavenly Father works much the same way. He patiently keeps chipping away and molding us to the image of His Son until we give a full commitment to Him.

> WHEN THE HEART FINDS ITS DELIGHT IN CHRIST ALONE, IT SOARS...

Just as our relationship with our children takes consistent cultivation, so will our relationship with Jesus. If we want to experience the delight and rapture of a life committed to Christ, we are the ones responsible to see that it happens. It's the promise of Jesus that when a heart hungers and thirsts for righteousness, it shall be filled!

So when the heart finds its delight in Christ alone, it soars above the strife of a vain and tempestuous world to worship where angels bow low and seraphim repeat their adoration to the One and only King. Amidst disappointments and struggle, the spirit can soar with eagles if it knows in whom to place its trust. Smiles during times of testing, perseverance when feelings are low, praise in moments of despair—these are possible when Christ becomes your longing and song.

Lord, search my heart for any unrest. Lead me in Your will and way. May I see and then submit. You have shown me that submission brings delight. Struggle only brings discontent and sorrow. I submit today to Your mercy and love. What delight to serve the King!

Perfect submission, perfect delight,
Visions of rapture now burst on my sight;
Angels descending bring from above
Echoes of mercy, whispers of love.

This is my story, this is my song,
Praising my Savior, all the day long;
This is my story, this is my song,
Praising my Savior, all the day long.

17

SOME THOUGHTS

- Ask the Father to increase your hunger for Him
- Commit yourself to Christ and His will again today
- Determine to truly worship Him through a life of praise

Day 8

Blessed Assurance

Perfect submission, all is at rest
I in my Savior am happy and blest,
Watching and waiting, looking above,
Filled with His goodness, lost in His love.

This is my story, this is my song,
Praising my Savior, all the day long;
This is my story, this is my song,
Praising my Savior, all the day long.

In our efforts to hold on to personal ambition without Christ, we miss the contentment that comes with abiding in Him. Thinking we'll find fulfillment, we race through life hoarding all that pleases, comforts, or entertains. We analyze every angle of personal worth and claim the right to wield our talents and goals for our own carnal desires. Like stubborn little children, we act like the Creator might misuse what He has created. In an effort to try to balance our personal space with God's will, we take pride in church attendance, good works, tithe, and other worthy tasks. Much to our dismay, instead of being fulfilled, we are miserable, irritable, and confused about our relationship with Christ.

It is at the point of full surrender that we find the fulfillment in life that before seemed so impossible. That which seems legitimate to us and that which seems foolish must all be laid before the Master. To find a satisfied, joyful saint, is to find one who has laid his/her all in the hands of God and continues to do this in total obedience. It is this type of vessel that God can do with as He pleases. Personal ambitions, goals, and desires are not driven by selfish motive but by what brings the greater glory to God.

This place of contentment in Christ does not make us extraterrestrial or some super human spiritual role model; it simply allows us to walk with Christ in the way He intended. Life moves on, disappointments come, temptations still arise, and the Christian keeps walking by faith content to be a follower of Christ. Lost in the love of God, he has no tolerance for the clamor of the world or the enemy's traps – He's satisfied with Jesus.

Sovereign Lord, I remember a moment when I fully surrendered forever. What rest and glory. You complete me. Your will defines me. Only in You do I find perfect peace.

Lord of my heart, lead me in surrender today. I trust Your plan. I submit to Your desire. Lead me in that submission.

I Am Thine, O Lord

CD Track: 4

I have met some wonderful saints in my lifetime, some of them Christian workers, others laymen, some missionaries, etc…. One wonders how they came so apparently close to Jesus. I have decided that there are some basic steps that will help all of us deepen our relationship with God.

> THERE IS NOTHING THAT I NEED THAT YOUR WILL CANNOT SUPPLY.

There is an urgency that comes from within that touches the heart of the Father when we get truly hungry or thirsty for Him. There's nothing better than drinking a cold glass of water or iced tea when we are thirsty, and there is nothing like the presence of Jesus for a dry thirsty soul. As the body craves nourishment for life, the spirit must crave fulfillment and life in Jesus. Like a father wants to give his children what they need, our Heavenly Father is waiting to fill a hunger if we just ask.

Some decisions and disciplines have to be grounded in our lives. The decision not to allow feelings to be the barometer for spiritual maturity or circumstances to dictate one's outlook on life is a start in the right direction. Determination to be spiritual amidst temptation and the every day grind of life is mandatory. When God sees our efforts to give our lives to Him, He rewards us with His presence, which in return fans a fire of hunger for more of Him.

If you're feeling like you're not sure where to start in wanting to be closer to Jesus, try a little experiment.

Be honest with God about your heart and where you are right now and then ask Him to make you hungry and thirsty for more of Him.

Pray the prayer every day and see what happens to your inner spirit.

You are the One who can fill all my longings,
There is nothing that I need that Your will cannot supply.
Allow my hunger for You to be my greatest desire,
Then satisfy that desire with Your presence.
Draw me near to Your heart and shut me in with You,
That I may please You with all my actions, thoughts, and plans.

I am Thine, O Lord, I have heard Thy voice,
And it told Thy love to me;
But I long to rise in the arms of faith
And be closer drawn to Thee.

Draw me nearer, nearer blessed Lord,
To the cross where Thou hast died.
Draw me nearer, nearer, nearer blessed Lord,
To Thy precious, bleeding side.

19

Day 10

I Am Thine, O Lord

Consecrate me now to Thy service, Lord,
By the power of grace divine;
Let my soul look up with a steadfast hope,
And my will be lost in Thine.

Draw me nearer, nearer blessed Lord,
To the cross where Thou hast died.
Draw me nearer, nearer, nearer blessed Lord,
To Thy precious, bleeding side.

There are crossroads that mark our lives – the pivotal moments where dreams, goals, and ambitions meet up with eternal destiny. Some of these crossroads have a greater significance than others, but all are important. As His children we analyze these life decisions based upon the perplexing question, "Is this God's will for me?" It is at this point we begin the quest to find the answer, seek the correct path, etc....

ULTIMATE GOAL.... GOD'S GLORY

The consolation prize is culminated in the earnest desire and prayer that our lives be totally consecrated to Jesus. It is at this marker we can return to a life that is incredibly complicated or hard to understand. Though our expectations of being able to discern the will of God are positive, the zeal of pursuit is often hindered by a cacophony of hindrances. Humanly, we try to measure up with peers and the decisions they have made to be successful. Spiritually, we struggle to know if we are truly "spiritual" enough to make the "right" decision. Emotionally, we battle despair of ever being what we would love to be for God's glory. Honestly, these moments are loaded with decisions that tell us much about ourselves and frequently alter the course of our lives. It's in these times when we place our trust in God that He understands our heart's motive and desire rather than our human wisdom or ability.

The ultimate goal at every crossroad is to determine what will bring the greater glory to God. It's not about us. It's about Him. And when we lose focus of that, we make unwise decisions and half-hearted blunders. The opportune moments life brings, whether good or bad, are our chance to give our best for the glory of God.

SING OR SPEAK TODAY'S VERSE AND CHORUS AS A PRAYER

Savior of my heart,

*There is nothing in me that has earned the right to serve You. I am not worthy to
perform Your work.*

*It is Your grace that sets me apart to be used. May that grace bind me to Your will alone.
Your grace gives my heart the eyes of faith to hope in You. Make Thy will mine today. Amen.*

Day 11

CD Track: 4

I Am Thine, O Lord

WHEN THOU SAIDST, SEEK YE MY FACE; MY HEART SAID UNTO THEE, THY FACE, LORD, WILL I SEEK. PSALM 27:8

O the pure delight of a single hour
That before Thy throne I spend,
When I kneel in prayer, and with Thee,
my God
I commune as friend with friend!

Draw me nearer, nearer blessed Lord,
To the cross where Thou hast died.
Draw me nearer, nearer, nearer blessed Lord,
To Thy precious, bleeding side.

The struggles between the rat race of life and the discipline to spend time alone with God make this stanza a little more difficult to sing. By the time we meet one deadline, there is another in its place. The children have practices, classes, meals, laundry, and a host of other stuff that need attending…. Work schedules and home demands don't stop…. Financial mountains, social discomforts, and high-pressure decisions are still hurling themselves at us in record-breaking speed…. Vacations, shopping, and socializing are inviting and sometimes necessary…. All of life would consume our every minute if we would let it!

No matter what our excuses or demands in life, failure to spend time alone with Jesus leads to dissatisfaction spiritually. This in turn touches every facet of our lives. We can quickly become irritable, spiritually indifferent, and a prime target for temptation! Good people are starving themselves and failing spiritually due to lack of commitment to their devotional time. This is the first area Satan will attack. He knows it's your spiritual lifeline.

More than fewer find time with God is first a discipline before it becomes a delight. A determined spirit is required to faithfully meet with God. Diligence and perseverance with our devotions are rewarded with the delight of His personal communion in our daily lives. This communion is found in prayer, scripture, song, quiet contemplation, sermons, and other spiritual venues.

A DETERMINED SPIRIT IS REQUIRED TO FAITHFULLY MEET WITH GOD.

The great thing is that, no matter what our personal goals for prayer length or reading habits, He takes note of every second we devote to Him. Lack of feeling or sensing His presence in prayer is no indication of His absence. The key is to keep praying – honestly and earnestly.

God is so faithful to remind us, to patiently lead us, and to nudge us toward our quiet time. We don't always get it right in our efforts to walk with God. Yet He is there waiting for us to grow, mature, and come to Him. Feel like you've been a failure? Run back to Him. He's rooting for you to get back up, put your hand to the plow, and keep going!

This time alone with Jesus
* O, how it keeps my soul*
From vanity, fear, and failure
* In Him I am made whole*

I do not need to question
* How he would have me be*
When I have learned to know Him
* And heeded faithfully*

The love of Christ my Savior
* Flows freely in my life*
His presence shines more clearly
* Amidst the struggles and the strife*

It is delight to abide in Him
* He leads so patiently*
I trust my friend with all my cares
* He is holy, true, and kind*

Day 12

Tell Me the Story of Jesus

Tell me the story of Jesus,
Write on my heart every word.
Tell me the story most precious,
Sweetest that ever was heard.

Tell how the angels in chorus,
Sang as they welcomed His birth.
"Glory to God in the highest!
Peace and good tidings to earth."

Tell me the story of Jesus,
Write on my heart every word.
Tell me the story most precious,
Sweetest that ever was heard.

I think I truly began to associate this song with Christmas when I began to have children of my own at home. I have always loved the time of year with presents, nativities, trees and lights, Christmas pageantry, holiday music, lots of sweets, huge meals….it's awesome! Christmas is my favorite time of year. However, since I have three gorgeous little girls, Christmas is about them, a lot less about me, and making sure they know it's all about Him. Since I collect nativities, it's a big deal at Christmas to get them all out and set them all over the house. This provides a great opportunity for my wife and I to tell the story again and again….I never get tired of it.

I love the rapture in their eyes when we speak of angels, animals, shepherds, Mary and Joseph, and the baby Jesus. Due to a tradition shared by some very dear friends of ours, the Jesus figurines that come out of the mangers are put away until Christmas morning. Before anything else happens Christmas day, my wife takes the girls through the house and places the babes into each nativity while I tell the story yet again.

The reason I love to tell my children this story was placed within my heart by my parents. My parents are first generation believers, and they knew little to nothing of the true meaning of Christmas while they were growing up. After their conversion they began their journey of telling the story again and again to us kids determined we would always understand the Story.

I love the story of Jesus, and I will forever tell it as long as He gives me breath and ability. Through song and testimony the wonders of his love will I share for His glory. It's the most amazing, most miraculous, and sweetest story ever written.

- *Start your own tradition with family or friends for sharing the Gospel story*
- *Discover a new method to share the story with someone today*

Loneliness into Friendship
Strife into Peace
Hatred into Love
Despair into Hope
Anxiety into Trust
Death into Life Eternal

All these changes occur because of the story of a baby sent to earth. Royalty became simplicity which led to a life of sacrifice for people who would despise and reject Him. Thank You, God, for writing this story of all stories to send Your dear Son to us. Amen.

Day 13

Tell Me the Story of Jesus

FOR WE HAVE NOT AN HIGH PRIEST WHICH CANNOT BE TOUCHED WITH THE FEELING OF OUR INFIRMITIES; BUT WAS IN ALL POINTS TEMPTED LIKE AS WE ARE, YET WITHOUT SIN. LET US THEREFORE COME BOLDLY UNTO THE THRONE OF GRACE, THAT WE MAY OBTAIN MERCY, AND FIND GRACE TO HELP IN TIME OF NEED. HEBREWS 4:15,16

Fasting alone in the desert,
  Tell of the days that are past.
How for our sins He was tempted,
  Yet was triumphant at last.

Tell of the years of His labor,
  Tell of the sorrow He bore.
He was despised and afflicted,
  Homeless, rejected and poor.

Tell me the story of Jesus,
  Write on my heart every word.
Tell me the story most precious,
  Sweetest that ever was heard.

My journey of reading about the life and ministry of Jesus through His Word and other writings from men of great credibility has been one of wonder and fascination at the very real way He came to this earth. The story is full of relationships, compassionate sacrifice, and deep love. The historical photos of the Christ with the bright aura of light around his head found in our large family Bible began to fade when I began to study the Gospel story for myself. It's more than angel's songs, heavenly visitations, dreams, and miraculous healings. It is the culmination of every word recorded in the Old and New Testaments. The whole Holy Bible is about Him.

When trying to comprehend the humanity of Christ, I notice the simple way He came to earth and dwelt among the poor, the common, the sick, and anyone else who would listen. My thoughts are amazed that the Creator became creation – immortal became human. I notice the enjoyment of wedding feasts, the trials of dusty trails, and the loss of a dear friend. I see the need for fellowship, the hunger felt from a fast, the weakness from hard work, and the need of a good sleep. Jesus came to be one of us to show us we can live a life that will please the Father.

His sacrificial love and compassion was shown not only in the cross, but also through His every day living as the ultimate example of a servant leader. The scriptures tell us over and over about His loving compassion demonstrated in the lives of the sinful and scorned, and his acts of mercy portrayed to them in His words and actions. The children were drawn to Him, the sinful received forgiveness, and the rejected found a friend. He healed their sick, walked miles to share His message, taught full long days, prayed through the nights, fasted for His ministry, and lived among the lowliest. He touched the lepers and the blind beggars, he went out of his way to talk to a Samaritan woman and others of ill repute, and He cast out devils. He denied any claim to fame or fortune, endured false accusations, scorned religious hypocrisy, and bore the mark of a fugitive. He paid the ultimate sacrifice when the sins of the whole world he willingly took upon himself and died the death of a criminal.

His story is the greatest love story ever written. Tell it again and again....

Day 14

Tell Me the Story of Jesus

Tell of the cross where they nailed Him,
  Writhing in anguish and pain.
Tell of the grave where they laid Him,
  Tell how He liveth again.

Love in that story so tender,
  Clearer than ever I see.
Stay, let me weep while you whisper,
  Love paid the ransom for me.

Tell me the story of Jesus,
  Write on my heart every word.
Tell me the story most precious,
  Sweetest that ever was heard.

Dramatic accounts of His suffering and death have paled in the reality that God became sin. Christian theologians, historians, musicians, poets, artists, philosophers, etc., have spent their entire lives trying to portray the pathos and triumph of the death and resurrection of Jesus. Others before Christ and since have suffered pain until death, but there could only be one spotless lamb to bear the reproach of every sin committed. Your sin and mine He bore that we might be free from the bondage of sin forever!

Amid the darkest hour on earth, the work of eternal business that was settled before time began was under way. The earth groaned and shook as it travailed under the mighty power of what had taken place on Calvary. One who bore it all to give life to countless millions who would find forgiveness through the blood shed for them was taking the defeat of death, sin, and hell captive. The echo of the announcement from the angel resounds even now, "He is not here, for He is risen as He said!"

The mystery of His life, death, and resurrection is overcome by a simple act of faith. No one, no matter how wise or intellectual, can describe all the ramifications of the story of Christ. Yet, even a child can understand the plan of Salvation that Jesus brings. The story is told again and again from the platforms of stadiums, shared in humble sanctuaries, resounded in high cathedrals, and presented with simple flannel graph stories. It's His story. Have you ever tried to tell it?

O Lord,
This is the story — Love Divine
  That takes a sinful heart like mine
And loves enough to writhe in pain
  To bear the ugly and bitter stain
Of full rejection of all that's good
  And see His Father turn His head

This love draws my heart to You
  It helps my faith remain true
Your story redeems unworthy me
  Let me not forget Calvary

28

He Hideth My Soul

HE THAT DWELLETH IN THE SECRET PLACE OF THE MOST HIGH SHALL ABIDE
UNDER THE SHADOW OF THE ALMIGHTY. I WILL SAY OF THE LORD, HE IS MY REFUGE
AND MY FORTRESS: MY GOD; IN HIM WILL I TRUST. SURELY HE SHALL DELIVER THEE
FROM THE SNARE OF THE FOWLER, AND FROM THE NOISOME PESTILENCE.
HE SHALL COVER THEE WITH HIS FEATHERS, AND UNDER HIS WINGS SHALT THOU TRUST:
HIS TRUTH SHALL BE THY SHIELD AND BUCKLER. PSALMS 91:1 – 4

Peace can be elusive and, if worried about, destroyed altogether. Trouble or busyness comes, and we think if we can just take a moment to sit down, drink a cup of coffee, and read a book will be rejuvenated enough to get through the week. The time comes when we throw ourselves into an easy chair a couple of minutes before supper and hope that the kids will remain quiet enough to give us a few minutes of peace. More than likely, our minds become full of expectations, bills to be paid, a house that needs to be cleaned, trouble at work…. Oh for just a few minutes of peace! Thoughts of peaceful moments give way to anxiety, and all too many times, to the spirit of fear and hopelessness.

We tend to tie the peace of God to human feelings or tidbits of sentimentality that we have stored away in the secret rooms of our minds that are supposed to bring a sense of rest to our harried lives. Every warm and fuzzy illustration we have ever heard or read comes to mind and all we can do is focus on what we don't have—peace. What must be realized is that God is not in the pretty picture, the serene sparrow on the side of the rocky mountain, or the little lamb trotting through the flowered hillside. He is not necessarily found in special friendships, extended vacations, or a life of ease. The more we strive for the stuff that's supposed to bring our sense of "peace," the more we frustrate ourselves. All too many times, the peace of God is never a part of our daily lives. We simply don't ask.

A wonderful Savior is Jesus my Lord,
A wonderful Savior to me;
He hideth my soul in the cleft of the rock,
Where rivers of pleasure I see.

He hideth my soul in the cleft of the rock
That shadows a dry, thirsty land;
He hideth my life with the depths of His love,
And covers me there with His hand,
And covers me there with His hand.

29

Continued on the next page

Day 15

I'm convinced that the peace of God comes to those who live inside the secret place. The soul can find solace within the shadow of the grace of God. Time spent alone with Him on purpose in good times and bad. Then all of the warm and delightful stories, fun activities, and relaxation can then be an enhancement of His hand if we first spend enough time with Him to receive His grace into our lives.

Lead me to the secret place, and tell me of Your love.
  Hide me in the shelter of Your open arms of grace.
Keep me safe and keep me pure.
  I can rest and be secure,
Hiding safe inside Your will.
  Please, Lord, keep me still. Amen.

He Hideth My Soul

Day 16

CASTING ALL YOUR CARE UPON HIM; FOR HE CARETH FOR YOU.
I PETER 5:7

He means for it to be simple really. We complicate our guilt and burdens by hanging on to them or mulling them over in our minds till they drive us crazy. He wants us to trust Him just like a child trusts a parent to take care of him. Mom and Dad can sooth anything.

I remember as a child and even as an adolescent lying down at bedtime and feeling guilty of naughtiness done during the day or fearful about some topic or another. It wouldn't be long until I would crawl out of bed and go knock on my parents' door. My godly mother would come out and pray with me, talk with me, sometimes fix a snack, and then send me back to bed. I remember a time when I was letting the enemy run over my emotions concerning the security of my salvation. The frankness and, yes, stern voice of my father pulled me out of confusion and into the reality of God's love and forgiveness.

Why I stew, worry, and fret about the details of life when I have Jesus is because I am human, I guess. What I am trying to learn is to take my burdens to Him on a daily basis rather than hoard them up in my mind for endless days.

Too often, we chat more than we pray. Then we feel guilty and ask the Lord to forgive us for talking too much and totally miss the opportunity to really pray about the said concern. We tote it around some more…. To our dismay we cope with our emotions until we are discouraged and weak.

He still is inviting us to come….it doesn't matter how long it takes for us to get there. So we kneel in prayer and give our burdens to Him, and He is always there. Life can get tough and even downright mean, but we can make it if we are doing it with Him. He covers me with His hand…

Jesus, Your Word tells us that God has measured the heavens with a span and holds all the waters in the palm of His hand.

My children are amazed at hands that big. I am amazed at love so great!

How can I doubt that You can take my burdens? Who but You could hold me up? What greater strength could ever be found?

I praise You for the covering and comfort of Your hand. Amen.

A Wonderful Savior is Jesus my Lord
He taketh my burden away
He holdeth me up and I shall not be moved
He giveth me strength as my day.

He hideth my soul in the cleft of the rock
That shadows a dry, thirsty land;
He hideth my life with the depths of His love,
And covers me there with His hand,
And covers me there with His hand.

31

Day 17

He Hideth My Soul

With numberless blessings each
moment He crowns,
And filled with His fullness divine,
I sing in my rapture, oh, glory to God
For such a Redeemer as mine!

He hideth my soul in the cleft of the rock
That shadows a dry, thirsty land;
He hideth my life with the depths
of His love,
And covers me there with His hand,
And covers me there with His hand.

I love to read the book of Psalms. David knew how to express himself, and his musician's heart is poured out into script. This shepherd warrior bares his inner soul as he pours forth anguish, anger, praise, worship, and thanksgiving. I don't have to read long before I find something that lifts my spirit. This guy knew how to praise the Lord. Physical and emotional, individual and corporate worship are laid out both in example and instruction. God honored his open and transparent heart and made him one of the greatest Kings that ever lived.

We could learn to be overwhelmed by God's goodness. It takes practice and total reliance upon God, but we can become a part of the praise team. We should do a weekly, if not daily, account of how good God is to us. "Numberless blessings" – have you tried to count them lately? In the downers of life, there is nothing like looking up and truly seeing the goodness from God's hand. If we are going to be filled with God's blessing we have to exercise our right to praise Him. The more we praise the more He honors and bestows His grace into our lives.

Fanny Crosby writes, "He hideth my life in the depths of His love." The picture I get here is "totally immersed" in the love of God. This acknowledgement teaches that His love reaches far past the here and now to actually what prepares me for Heaven. When we immerse ourselves in His goodness, we are too full of Him to desire any earthly good.

LEARN TO BE OVERWHELMED BY GOD'S GOODNESS

Sometimes I am overwhelmed by Your care. So many little blessings I do not deserve: the mercies that are new every day, the promise to hear my whispered prayer, and the protection and peace You provide.

How can I keep from sharing Your goodness? How can I worry as if You are not there? The covering of Your hand comforts and corrects me. Your dwelling surrounds me with joy, and in Your secret place I long to stay. Amen.

He Hideth My Soul

REJOICE, BECAUSE YOUR NAMES ARE WRITTEN IN HEAVEN.
LUKE 10:20B

Fanny Crosby's songs almost always give way to the promise of Heaven. There is an expectancy of the promise from Jesus that He has gone to prepare us a place!

You can feel the urgency of some of these old songwriters as they lived for another place other than "the here and now." This kind of expectant faith lends itself to a close relationship with Jesus, and is really the spirit of the New Testament. Jesus words were to "Watch and Pray!" This kind of anticipation lends itself toward careful living, doing good deeds, loving your neighbor, and all that comes with living a life that is pleasing to God.

Jesus told us that we should rejoice to know that our names have been written in the Book of Life! If we are not careful, we allow the clouds of this world to block the view of the other side completely. This is going to happen from time to time, but if we keep walking, He'll clear the way. The more we walk and talk with Him, the less this old world tugs at our hearts strings.

HANG ONTO THE HOPE!

Hope of heaven
  Hope of life
Hope that leads beyond the strife
  Hope that keeps me here below
Hope that leads to Heaven's shore

Doubt and dark despair
  Sin will take me there.
A nail-scarred hand is reaching down.
  This hand leads me to the light.
This love takes away my night.

Hope of heaven – Eternal rest
  There my heart is truly home.

*When clothed in His brightness, transported
I rise
  To meet Him in clouds of the sky,
His perfect salvation, His wonderful love
  I'll shout with the millions on high.*

*He hideth my soul in the cleft of the rock
  That shadows a dry, thirsty land;
He hideth my life with the depths of His love,
  And covers me there with His hand,
And covers me there with His hand.*

33

Day 19

To God Be The Glory

FOR GOD SO LOVED THE WORLD THAT HE GAVE HIS ONLY BEGOTTEN SON; THAT
WHOSOEVER BELIEVETH IN HIM SHOULD NOT PERISH, BUT HAVE EVERLASTING LIFE.
JOHN 3:16

To God be the glory,

great things He has done;

So loved He the world

that He gave us His Son,

Who yielded His life an atonement for sin,

And opened the life gate that all may go in.

Praise the Lord, praise the Lord,

Let the earth hear His voice!

Praise the Lord, praise the Lord,

Let the people rejoice!

O come to the Father,

through Jesus the Son,

And give Him the glory,

great things He has done.

The greatest of all sacrifices was culminated in the death of God's Son for a fallen race. Provision for forgiveness of sins was granted to every man, woman, boy, and girl through the blood of Jesus Christ. The death of Christ made possible the way into the Holy of Holies where all can find God's mercy, forgiveness, and restoration. We, who could do nothing to help our own plight, have been redeemed, washed in the blood, forgiven, made a new creation! Praise the Lord!

Begin a journey of praise in your life. Look around you at what God has done. Start with the realization of salvation in your own life, and then talk to your fellow believers at church or small group study about their testimonies and share your own. Turn on the radio and, on purpose, listen to a Christian radio broadcast that shares what God is doing around the world in bringing people to himself. God is doing great things in the world today! Make sure you are on the praise committee!

We have not been given the vocabulary rich enough to praise You. We try to give thanks in humble, stumbling words. Accept our offerings, though too small, and know they come from hearts that yearn to know Your glory, to feel Your presence, and to give You praise due to Your name.

To God Be The Glory

IF WE CONFESS OUR SINS, HE IS FAITHFUL AND JUST TO FORGIVE US OUR SINS,
AND TO CLEANSE US FROM ALL UNRIGHTEOUSNESS. 1 JOHN 1:9

Many people struggle with their pasts. Haunting memories of what used to be still plaguing their dreams and clouding their future. It's difficult to focus on the new start Christ brings when the scars run deep into the soul. Failure to meet the mark in the past makes it seem impossible to be anything better in the future.

If it were not for God's grace, we couldn't make it. Deeper than the stain of sin could ever go, God's love, mercy, and forgiveness go deeper still. Bringing healing and restoration, He makes it possible for a new start, and is able to complete it until He calls us home.

It's easy for us to compare ourselves with those who appear to be a success in ministry or who have made wise choices in their lives and families. It doesn't hurt us to want to be better people, but we can't wallow in what we cannot choose again. We would be much better off to find some redemptive stories from God's Word to be our guide. Read of David, Paul, Rahab, Samson, and others who found grace in spite of life choices that are less than ideal.

Learn to give God praise where you are right now. Don't let the regrets and disappointments of life keep you from going forward.

- Praise Him for what He has done so far in your life.
- Praise Him for being merciful.
- Praise Him for where He wants to take you.
- Praise Him because your name is written in the Lamb's Book of life.

Merciful Redeemer, Let me not forget just how costly the act of Your love. Remind me of the change You have made in my heart. Thank You for a clear pardon and a new beginning. I rejoice in You and give You glory. Amen.

O perfect redemption, the purchase of blood,
To every believer the promise of God;
The vilest offender who truly believes,
That moment from Jesus a pardon receives.

Praise the Lord, praise the Lord,
Let the earth hear His voice!
Praise the Lord, praise the Lord,
Let the people rejoice!
O come to the Father, through Jesus the Son,
And give Him the glory,
great things He has done.

35

Day 21

Rescue the Perishing

AND WHEN THE SCRIBES AND PHARISEES SAW HIM EAT WITH PUBLICANS AND SINNERS, THEY SAID UNTO HIS DISCIPLES, HOW IS IT THAT HE EATETH AND DRINKETH WITH PUBLICANS AND SINNERS? WHEN JESUS HEARD IT, HE SAITH UNTO THEM, THEY THAT ARE WHOLE HAVE NO NEED OF THE PHYSICIAN, BUT THEY THAT ARE SICK: I CAME NOT TO CALL THE RIGHTEOUS, BUT SINNERS TO REPENTANCE. MARK 2:16,17

Rescue the perishing, care for the dying,
Snatch them in pity
from sin and the grave;
Weep o'er the erring one, lift up the fallen,
Tell them of Jesus, the mighty to save.

Rescue the perishing, care for the dying,
Jesus is merciful, Jesus will save.

Though they are slighting Him,
still He is waiting,
Waiting the penitent child to receive;
Plead with them earnestly,
plead with them gently;
He will forgive if they only believe.

When I was a young man, my church sent some of us teens over to South Africa on a mission's trip. Though we were full of adolescent behavior and immaturity, the mission's trip made a significant impact upon my life. Six weeks out of a summer can provide a lot of memories for a young person. We sang, gave testimony, preached, told Bible stories, walked, and ate little.

Out of all the memories from that particular visit, I remember the commitment to serving others that I saw from that elderly couple. He was hard of hearing and she found it difficult to see; and neither one of them were "good" with the language. Yet they pursued and used what they had for God. It was no small work they were doing either. They ran us young people to death!

Early in the morning we could hear them in their prayer closets calling out to God for His blessing on their ministry. They did not count themselves as heroes or great warriors of faith; they were just giving of themselves to God. I'm convinced the prayer they gave themselves to gave them the strength to do the work of rescuing the perishing.

During a summer of traveling, my family was providing music at a small camp in southern Indiana where a young black man came through singing for a Bible college group. Through his testimony and talking with him after the service, I found out he was

RESCUE THE PERISHING MAY NOT CALL YOU ACROSS THE WATERS OR TO FOREIGN FIELDS, BUT IT WILL REQUIRE SOMETHING VERY DEAR — YOURSELF.

36

one of the products of the dear missionary couple in South Africa. He was attending their services ten to fifteen years ago as a small child when I was there with the mission's team.

Rescue the perishing may not call you across the waters or to foreign fields, but it will require something very dear – yourself. You must care. You must give. You must go as He bids. It's not about being a hero or having your biography printed in hardback and sold at the local bookstore. It's about giving of yourself to God and others in love.

Help me see all the lost today
Running blindly on their way
Show me the scars You wear for me
That I might point the lost to thee

Give me the words to heal their pain
Grant me love to once again
Look beyond their sin and shame
To see the soul You died to claim

Day 22

Rescue the Perishing

BUT WHEN HE SAW THE MULTITUDES, HE WAS MOVED WITH COMPASSION ON THEM, BECAUSE THEY FAINTED, AND WERE SCATTERED ABROAD, AS SHEEP HAVING NO SHEPHERD. THEN SAITH HE UNTO HIS DISCIPLES, THE HARVEST TRULY IS PLENTEOUS, BUT THE LABOURERS ARE FEW; PRAY YE THEREFORE THE LORD OF THE HARVEST, THAT HE WILL SEND FORTH LABOURERS INTO HIS HARVEST. MATTHEW 9:36 – 38

Down in the human heart,

crushed by the tempter,

  Feelings lie buried that grace can restore;

Touched by a loving heart,

wakened by kindness,

  Chords that were broken

  will vibrate once more.

Rescue the perishing, care for the dying,

  Jesus is merciful, Jesus will save.

Rescue the perishing, duty demands it;

  Strength for thy labor

  the Lord will provide;

Back to the narrow way patiently win them;

  Tell the poor wand'rer a Savior has died.

Tired?

Worn out from all the stuff life brings? Weary from doing even "good" stuff?

Amid the busyness of life, it's amazing how quick we can wear ourselves out! No matter what vocation you work or where life has left you at the moment, you're probably busier than you want to be. Mix in a little disappointment here, trial there, car trouble, bills, and life's rat race, and you've got a job to manage it all and still keep some type of sanity and mooring to your spiritual life. This stuff happens if you're a plumber or a preacher, teacher or a politician, missionary or a gas attendant – it just don't matter! We all have the "stuff" oozing out of our lives!

So we take the time to go to a revival, conference, or retreat, and we hear truth on how we need to be caring a burden for the lost, working harder for Jesus, and giving more of our time to God. I'm afraid that more people leave frustrated, befuddled, and maybe a little skeptical at what level the speaker understands real life, rather than leaving convicted. Others leave so overwhelmed by life and by the need that they excuse themselves from responsibility and simply don't do anything. What's the answer to this madness?

I think a key component is compassion – honestly and earnestly seeking the heart of God for a better understanding of how He views His creation. Compassion is love in action. It's the cure for an ailing spirit and a broken heart. It's what Jesus lived.

Jesus understands "tired." Jesus realizes human limitations. Jesus also has a place for you to serve. He can see the strengths and weaknesses of each individual and has the ability to help us respond the way He wants.

These could be a few ideas to start praying about:

- To see a need and respond
- To hurt when others do
- To listen and do less talking
- To focus on a friend's need when feeling lonely or depressed
- To make family a priority
- To visit a rest home or an assisted living
- To ask your pastor about a chore or visitation program

....He didn't ask us to do something we couldn't do. He asks us to do exactly what we can...so how is it you need to pray today?

Jesus, Help me to carry Your burden for souls. May I see the lost as Your loved, lost lambs. Help my compassion to match Yours. Give me divine love that never ends. Grant me some soul today. Make me faithful to the things of eternal value that I might be ready to draw the perishing into the lifeboat of grace. Amen.

Day 23

Unsearchable Riches

UNTO ME, WHO AM LESS THAN THE LEAST OF ALL SAINTS, IS THIS GRACE GIVEN,
THAT I SHOULD PREACH AMONG THE GENTILES THE UNSEARCHABLE RICHES OF CHRIST.
EPHESIANS 3:8

Oh, the unsearchable riches of Christ,
Wealth that can never be told!
Riches exhaustless of mercy and grace,
Precious, more precious than gold.

Precious more precious,
Wealth that can never be told!
Oh, the unsearchable riches of Christ!
Precious, more precious than gold.

Oh, the unsearchable riches of Christ!
Who shall their greatness declare?
Jewels whose luster our lives may adorn,
Pearls that the poorest may wear!

Who can deny the adventurous spirit that calls to most of us at some time or another to step out and take the challenge into the unknown? History bears witness to the now unmarked paths of early pioneers and settlers looking for a new beginning. Brave stories of diligence, sacrifice, and primitive living conditions testify to the unrestrained faith for something better. Pursuits of gold, land, freedom, and adventures of all kinds fill our museums and history books reminding us of the great, unknown journey of life.

The quest is on! Continual searching for the adventure of life is as ritualistic as the beat of man's heart. The pursuit of hobbies, success, and adventure in and of itself can be and is healthy for positive living. Pity is to be taken on those who cannot find any reason to live life to its fullest potential.

Due to the fact that fulfillment outside of Christ is an impossibility, enticement of adventuring into the unknown has a downside. The spirit of the universe does not lend itself toward the moral and holy. The consequences to the unabated passions of those in quest of life's adventure are wreaking havoc in not only the church but also general society. The prognosis of life without the true value of relationship found in Christ is at best disappointing and, in the end, damning.

IF YOU KNOW CHRIST, YOUR ADVENTURE WILL LEAD YOU IN DIRECTIONS YOU NEVER DREAMED POSSIBLE!

40

Those who profess to know Christ have foundationally taken their proverbial leaps of faith into the realm of total confidence in the security of God's Word. Everything in life becomes measured by the rich truth found in its pages. Genuine relationship is started between a man and his God. It's not rational, and it's not understood without the eyes of faith. Through life challenges, hardships, and blessings he hangs onto the confidence that the new beginning once started is completing its responsibility to conform him into the image of His Creator.

Though he cannot see, he must believe.

Though he cannot feel, he must trust.

Though he cannot humanly reason, he must hold on.

Though he cannot fathom God's love, he must rest in its promise.

Hang on tight! If you know Christ, your adventure will lead you in directions you never dreamed possible! As Christ becomes all you need, deep fulfillment and longings are found. There is no need to keep on looking. He becomes the greatest treasure of all.

Make a list of your greatest expectations in life.

• Do they measure up to the truth of God's Word?

• Pray right now about your desire to have a truly God-driven life!

O, that I might nurture the desire to know You, Lord. Keep me ever in Your Word. Teach me truths that span the ages. Guide me in Your ways. Sharpen my soul so I will sense worldly things and keep far from them. Immerse me in the wondrous riches of Christ! Amen.

Day 24

CD Track: 10

Safe in the arms of Jesus,
Safe on His gentle breast,
There by his love o' ershaded
Sweetly my soul shall rest.
Hark! 'tis the voice of angels,
Borne in a song to me.
Over the fields of glory,
Over the jasper sea.

Safe in the arms of Jesus,
Safe on His gentle breast
There by His love o'ershaded,
Sweetly my soul shall rest.

Safe in the arms of Jesus,
Safe from corroding care
Safe from the world's temptations,
Sin cannot harm me there.
Free from the blight of sorrow,
Free from my doubts and fears;
Only a few more trials,
Only a few more tears!

Jesus, my heart's dear Refuge,
Jesus has died for me;
Firm on the Rock of Ages,
Ever my trust shall be.
Here let me wait with patience,
Wait till the night is over;
Wait till I see the morning
Break on the golden shore.

Safe in the Arms of Jesus

I WILL BOTH LAY ME DOWN IN PEACE, AND SLEEP: FOR THOU, LORD, ONLY MAKEST ME DWELL IN SAFETY. PSALM 4:8

These are days when a sense of security eludes more than not and when found is a wonderful thing. Our place in history is one of war, financial instability, and spiritual unawareness. Families every day receive the news that a loved one has departed while defending freedoms. Hard working men and women who have worked for tenure and financial stability are given the notice they are no longer needed due to budget decreases. Humanistic philosophical thinking, godless education, and a decreased value of human life have left our nation with basically no moral compass. Security is hard to find.

Without the hope of a celestial refuge, there is really no security to be found. For every good that man possesses comes from the hands of the Creator. The security found in the arms of the everlasting God through a relationship built on the faith found in His word is the ultimate solace. His promise is to be with us always, even until the end of the age.

The most beautiful thing about a hug is the security of belonging one feels. That sense of love and warmth speaks volumes to friends, co-workers, and companions. In times of great celebration and times of loss, a touch means so much.

The arms of Jesus stand wide open in life and in death. Compassion is His specialty, and since He knows all the details of every situation its not a phony or incomplete sense of guilt or emotion, He truly cares. So, rest in the Lord, He'll securely take you through.

May my spiritual eyes always see clearly the road that will lead me home.
May my feet seek that place of refuge and safety that ends the strife and leads to life.
May my arms not hold dear the temporal things of this life, but may I wait with expectation to be drawn into the arms of the Savior.
May my soul find its home in heaven.
Jesus, the Kind Shepherd, I rest in You as I travel this path through earth that leads to home. I trust in Your care and know You will carry me through. Amen.

Close To Thee

Day 25

CD Track: 11

MY FLESH AND MY HEART FAILETH: BUT GOD IS THE STRENGTH OF MY HEART, AND MY POR-
TION FOREVER. FOR, LO, THEY THAT ARE FAR FROM THEE SHALL PERISH: THOU HAST DE-
STROYED ALL THEM THAT GO A WHORING FROM THEE. BUT IT IS GOOD FOR ME TO DRAW
NEAR TO GOD: I HAVE PUT MY TRUST IN THE LORD GOD, THAT I MAY DECLARE ALL THY
WORKS. PSALM 73:26 – 28

Declaring to love Jesus is a good thing. Actually being willing to give dreams, ambitions, and desires for life and service is something all together different. This love relationship with Jesus is so much more than "feeling" like a believer. It's "living" the life of a believer.

Being "close" to God is difficult at best to imagine through human reasoning. Yet God has chosen us to walk with Him before the foundations of the world! His plan for you to be a part of the Kingdom was made possible with the death of Christ on the cross. So we don't look at this relationship through human reasoning. We have to walk this relationship by faith. We pray and commune with Him through the eyes of prayer and His word. Through this process of "worship" our spiritual sense is strengthened, and we yearn to walk deeper into His presence. The more we long for Him, the sweeter we find Him to dwell within us.

Father, Help this weary soul to find the strength to seek You more. Increase my thirst for godliness and purity. Show my heart true wisdom that I will desire You more. What a privilege to be Your child! Amen.

Thou my everlasting Portion,
More than friend or life to me,
All along my pilgrim journey,
Savior let me walk with Thee.

Close to Thee, close to Thee,
Close to Thee, close to Thee
All along my pilgrim journey,
Savior let me walk with Thee.

Not for ease or worldly pleasure,
Nor for fame my prayer shall be;
Gladly will I toil and suffer,
Only let me walk with Thee.

Close to Thee, close to Thee,
Close to Thee, close to Thee
Gladly will I toil and suffer,
Only let me walk with Thee.

Day 26

Redeemed How I Love to Proclaim It

EVEN THE RIGHTEOUSNESS OF GOD WHICH IS BY FAITH OF JESUS CHRIST UNTO ALL AND UPON ALL THEM THAT BELIEVE: FOR THERE IS NO DIFFERENCE: FOR ALL HAVE SINNED, AND COME SHORT OF THE GLORY OF GOD; BEING JUSTIFIED FREELY BY HIS GRACE THROUGH THE REDEMPTION THAT IS IN CHRIST JESUS. ROMANS 3:22 – 24

Redeemed, how I love to proclaim it!
Redeemed by the blood of the Lamb;
Redeemed through his infinite mercy,
His child and forever I am.

Redeemed, redeemed,
Redeemed by the blood of the Lamb;
Redeemed, redeemed.
His child and forever I am.

Redeemed and so happy in Jesus,
No language my rapture can tell;
I know that the light of His presence
With me doth continually dwell.

I think of my blessed Redeemer,
I think of Him all the day long;
I sing for I cannot be silent;
His love is the theme of my song.

Redemption. Unworthy humanity reconciled unto God Himself. This redemption sounds rather absurd and a little too good to be true. But that's what makes the price of Calvary's blood so miraculous. There has never been a man or woman born who was good enough to merit the redeeming power of the blood of Christ. It is freely given for those who ask!

Only those who have experienced God's redemption plan in a personal relationship with His Son can fully understand the depths of gratitude the redeemed proclaim. Angels and celestial beings cannot know; only those who have experienced the grace of God applied to their lives understand the meaning of being redeemed. The redeemed have been persecuted, burned at the stake, devoured by lions, undergone destitution, and been forsaken by family. They have walked faithfully through times of spiritual famine, been blessed in times of renewal, and have given their lives to sacrifice, service, and even poverty. The redeemed have kept their homes sheltered from the onslaught of wickedness, bitterness, and spiritual decline. For they have found the pearl of great price. They have been redeemed!

We who have understood the forgiveness of sins can become accustomed to the liberty found in Christ. If not careful, we'll let the thrill of knowing Christ be replaced with the dullness of ritual and monotony of religion. Through the act of being faithful we must let our hearts rejoice with such songs and script as Fanny Crosby gave us in her "Redeemed How I Love to Proclaim It!"

The redeeming power of Christ still works now and always will. Tell someone today what Christ has done for you. In word and in deed let your light shine, for you are a part of the Redeemed!

I am privileged to be redeemed! You have paid the price for my sin, my debt has been canceled, and I have been changed. Saved from eternal hell and set on a path to heaven, I am no more the devil's slave but a true love servant to the King. I will one day reign with Christ. I am a lost soul now found and adopted. I Am Redeemed! Amen.

Near The Cross

LOOKING UNTO JESUS THE AUTHOR AND FINISHER OF OUR FAITH;
WHO FOR THE JOY THAT WAS SET BEFORE HIM ENDURED THE CROSS,
DESPISING THE SHAME, AND IS SET DOWN AT THE RIGHT HAND OF THE THRONE OF GOD.
FOR CONSIDER HIM THAT ENDURED SUCH CONTRADICTION OF SINNERS AGAINST
HIMSELF, LEST YE BE WEARIED AND FAINT IN YOUR MINDS. HEBREWS 12:2,3

Keeping perspective in life is kin to remembering where you have been or what you used to be. When we refuse to acknowledge our past, we lose something of what or where we could be headed in the future. To dwell in the past is useless, but to learn, acknowledge, and keep moving on is something altogether different.

> TO DWELL IN THE PAST IS USELESS, BUT TO LEARN, ACKNOWLEDGE, AND KEEP MOVING ON IS SOMETHING ALTOGETHER DIFFERENT.

To never ponder your life before you knew Jesus is to forget the transformation of being "born again." I'm not referring to dwelling on specific sin, sorrows too great to drudge up, or any other habit, hurt, or infraction upon life. I am referring to remembering the difference between a life laden with guilt vs. a life with peace and contentment in Christ. I am referring to remembering the difference between a life dead in sin vs. a life with eternal bliss. This is what we must remember.

When we take the time in prayer to thank the Lord for His amazing power to change what we have been, reflection takes us to the cross where He bore our sins that we may have life. Without remembering what He has done, we grow lukewarm and discontent. We are human and it's easy to take anything for granted. The price He paid on Calvary can never be taken for granted.

So keep a right perspective. The next time you hear this song or sing it in church, don't let the song's tendency of slow tempo distract you from focusing on the purpose of the words Remember!

Lord Jesus, Thank You for the cross. Keep the price You paid before me that I forget not all You have done to give me life. Help me remember all Your pain when I tend to grumble about my life, and make me willing to bear Your cross. Help me to stay near this place so I will not forget Your grace. Amen.

Jesus, keep me near the cross,
There a precious fountain
Free to all, a healing stream
Flows from Calvary's mountain.

Near the cross, a trembling soul,
Love and mercy found me;
There the bright and morning star
Sheds its beams around me.

In the cross, in the cross,
Be my glory ever;
Till my raptured soul shall find
Rest beyond the river.

Near the cross! O Lamb of God,
Bring its scenes before me;
Help me walk from day to day,
With its shadows o'er me.

45

Day 28

My Savior First of All

When my life work is ended, and I cross the swelling tide,
When the bright and glorious morning
I shall see;
I shall know my Redeemer when I reach the other side,
And His smile will be the first to
welcome me.

I shall know Him, I shall know Him,
And redeemed by His side I shall stand,
I shall know Him, I shall know Him,
By the print of the nails in His hand.

Oh, the soul thrilling rapture when
I view His blessèd face,
And the luster of His kindly beaming eye;
How my full heart will praise Him for the mercy, love and grace,
That prepare for me a mansion in the sky.

I enjoy life. I enjoy the comforts of family and friends. I love my wife, my girls, and my life's occupation. I have healthy relationships with friends, and I get along with my peers at the work place. I won't bore you with any more optimistic points in my life, and I won't share all the negative issues either! Most can understand why at my age, life is not a drudgery or a bore.

I've tried to imagine a place better than this life. In my mind I can hear different preachers thunder forth eschatology and descriptions of the place called heaven. My mind begins to swim as my imagination tries to picture angels, streets of gold, millions of people, lush scenery, etc....

PERSPECTIVE

A few years ago, a traumatic accident in our home caused me to do some re-evaluating about life and brought the reality of heaven closer. When Mariah, our then 4 year old, was hit by an automobile right outside of our home, the reality of eternal value came knocking. Working too long hours even for good stuff became insignificant, and I realized the only earthly thing that mattered was my family and our relationship to God. With broken hearts we realized how close we came to giving back to God the most precious gift he had given to us. In those moments we felt the everlasting arms of God like never before, and we knew she would be in His care whatever His will would unfold to be. Perspective. It's amazing how a few moments in time change your life forever.

46

If life is good here with all its twists and turns, upheavals and headaches, blessings and triumphs, I want to share with everyone the advantage of God's grace to prepare for the day when we shall truly live! Time will cease to exist as we know it, and we shall be with Him. We will then understand the way He laid for us, for we shall be with Him forever.

Yes, I shall know Him
The One who makes me whole
Yes, I shall see Him
When I have reached my goal
Heaven – eternal joy and bliss

To think that the end of this life only opens the door to heaven! Keep me close to the Savior so that I die ready to meet Him!

I praise You for the promise of a future with You. Redeemer, I shall know You and will bow before You then as now. My greatest reward will be Your smile. Amen.

Day 29

CD Track: 14

My Savior First of All

AFTER THIS I BEHELD, AND, LO, A GREAT MULTITUDE, WHICH NO MAN COULD NUMBER, OF ALL NATIONS, AND KINDREDS, AND PEOPLE, AND TONGUES, STOOD BEFORE THE THRONE, AND BEFORE THE LAMB, CLOTHED WITH WHITE ROBES, AND PALMS IN THEIR HANDS. AND CRIED WITH A LOUD VOICE, SAYING, SALVATION TO OUR GOD WHICH SITTETH UPON THE THRONE, AND UNTO THE LAMB. AND ALL THE ANGELS STOOD ROUND ABOUT THE THRONE, AND ABOUT THE ELDERS AND THE FOUR BEASTS, AND FELL BEFORE THE THRONE ON THEIR FACES, AND WORSHIPPED GOD, SAYING, AMEN: BLESSING, AND GLORY, AND WISDOM, AND THANKSGIVING, AND HONOUR, AND POWER, AND MIGHT, BE UNTO OUR GOD FOR EVER AND EVER. AMEN. REVELATION 7:9 – 12

Oh, the dear ones in glory,
how they beckon me to come,
   And our parting at the river I recall;
To the sweet vales of Eden
they will sing my welcome home;
   But I long to meet my Savior first of all.

I shall know Him, I shall know Him,
   And redeemed by His side I shall stand,
I shall know Him, I shall know Him,
   By the print of the nails in His hand.

Through the gates to the city
in a robe of spotless white,
   He will lead me where no tears will ever fall;
In the glad song of ages
I shall mingle with delight;
   But I long to meet my Savior first of all.

There are moments of life that capture and leave a permanent print on our hearts. Simple, complicated, fun, hurtful, life has a way of bringing it all into focus.

As a Dad there are moments with the girls that I'm sure I will never forget. Pictures flow through my mind of carousel rides, messy ice cream cones, family fun nights, excitement at Christmas, and giggling pajama time. Moments treasured for life. These memories flow deep within us bringing to us a smile, a scent of hope for the future, and we know life is good.

Not all the pictures of life are captivating and inviting. Difficult moments of pain and disappointment that we try to forget or receive healing for also leave us different people. We all go through difficult times! It seems that God has a way of bringing people into our lives who show us how strong His grace can be for every difficulty that we endure.

Fresh out of college and working as a minister of music I had the privilege to know some very precious saints. One such missionary lady, who had endured much emotional and physical pain, would often report that she would know her Savior when she got Home. Her theme was that, through

OUR REACTIONS .... WILL BE IN THE CARE OF THE MASTER PRODUCER.

all the moments of life, she had learned to hear his voice, and she knew that she would not just see with her eyes the scars of crucifixion but she would know the voice of her Savior.

Eventually, the end of the film will happen for all of us. The story will be over, and the credits will be evident of how we spent our lives. Our reactions to the circumstances of life and what we did with what we had been given will be in the care of the Master Producer. It's at that moment that whatever we gave our lives to live for will be evident. The ultimate reward as we step out on streets of gold will be the face of the Redeemer. And I shall know Him.

How can I not know You when You walked beside me here?
You wrapped me in Your arms of love when shadows lingered near.
Your Word has been my constant guide and comfort day by day.
Your blessings have overwhelmed me daily.
How can I not know the One who bore my pain?
I long to see You through Your Word but someday face to face!

Day 30

Praise Him! Praise Him!

FROM THE RISING OF THE SUN UNTO THE GOING DOWN OF THE SAME
THE LORD'S NAME IS TO BE PRAISED. PSALM 113:3

Praise Him! Praise Him!
  Jesus, our blessed Redeemer!
Sing, O Earth,
  His wonderful love proclaim!
Hail Him! Hail Him!
  Highest archangels in glory;
Strength and honor
  Give to His holy Name!
Like a shepherd,
  Jesus will guard His children,
In His arms
  He carries them all day long:
Praise Him! Praise Him!
  Tell of His excellent greatness.
Praise Him! Praise Him!
  Ever in joyful song!

The scriptures are full of personal and corporate accounts of praise to God. Praise for victories won, praise for prayers answered, praise for miraculous works, etc. We can read personal exaltation and praise during times of good health and sickness, during times of war and peace, during times of spiritual renewal and times of struggle. Other accounts tell of national praise that resulted from great visitations from God to his chosen people.

There are examples of praise both in public and private settings. Isaiah, Jeremiah, Nehemiah, Ezekiel, and other prophets of old praised the Lord publicly during times of pagan influence and great persecution. Job learned to give praise privately during great loss and sickness. During times of miraculous healing people gave praise publicly while others quietly talked with the Savior. While in prison, Paul and Silas privately praised the Lord in song until the earth shook and their chains fell off.

Other accounts of worship and praise are given as a result of restoration between God and man, such as on Mt. Carmel when praise became mingled with holy reverence for a God who would send fire upon a sacrifice to change the course of a nation. Heathen cultures turned from their wicked ways to worship the God of heaven due to His power shown through human instruments such as David, Daniel, Esther, Elijah, Jonah, Paul, Steven, the disciples, and a host of others. The narratives given in Scripture record the praise of His people who had been reconciled unto Himself. We ought to be praising Him, too!

In the book of Revelation we read of seraphim, angels, and terrestrials that praise the eternal Father. They give constant and consistent praise to the Lamb who is worthy. The brightest of intellectuals try to comprehend the mysteries of adoration given spontaneously and ritualistically without ceasing before the throne of God. Such powerful examples make us feel very inadequate to praise the Lord as we ought. He is Holy. He is worthy to be praised.

All of this and more are given to show us that it is paramount we give praise to God. Jesus said that the rocks would begin to cry out if the people did not praise Him. Lift your spirit and lend your voice today to Praise the Lord!

"Let everything that hath breath, Praise the Lord!"

PRACTICAL APPLICATION:

- *Write a list of blessings – give God praise for each one*
- *Go through your ipod, mp3, or media player and create a new playlist of songs of praise from various artists*
- *Give audible praise to God in prayer*
- *Tell a friend or family member a specific praise to God*
- *Do a word search on "praise" in the Bible*
- *Start a praise journal of God's work in your life*

I take this time to praise You for all the things You've done.
I pause and am astounded by the goodness of Your hand.
I thank You for Your mercy, the grace, and love You've shown.
I offer all my life to You in worship at Your throne.

Day 31

Praise Him! Praise Him!

Praise Him! Praise Him!
Jesus, our blessed Redeemer!
For our sins
He suffered, and bled, and died.
He our Rock,
Our hope of eternal salvation,
Hail Him! Hail Him!
Jesus the Crucified.
Sound His praises!
Jesus who bore our sorrows,
Love unbounded,
Wonderful, deep and strong.
Praise Him! Praise Him!
Tell of His excellent greatness.
Praise Him! Praise Him!
Ever in joyful song!

52

Through two thousand years of history the Gospel story is still burning in the hearts of believers. Time has had no chains on the effectiveness of the Gospel. Through eras of religious popularity and persecution, faith in Christ and the Gospel message has remained the fortress for the Christian.

The journey has never been or ever will be easy as men consistently try to deny Christ's authenticity and global impact. Deceit, persecution, torture, imprisonment, and even death cannot annihilate the Gospel. In fact, the hope of eternal salvation has been spreading in greater and grander ways than ever before. Regardless of how the enemy endeavors to stamp out His light, God always has a people committed to giving everything they have, if necessary, to the cause of the Gospel.

The fervency found in the founding fathers' faith is still the bedrock for Christians today. It isn't shrouded in the merits of old phraseology or ancient tradition, but it is found in the honest hearts of twenty-first century believers who desire to please Him – men and women of faith who dare to stand for principle, Bible truth, and moral obligation. These are the people God will use to continue sounding forth His praises through the Gospel story.

We have a charge to keep the story of Christ and His love to the world. We have reason and cause to sing.

"Tell of His excellent greatness."

My heart stands in praise to a God who can do such wonderful things!
I am redeemed from destruction and eternal death and brought unto life and eternal bliss!
Hail the King of all Kings!
Hail the Son of God who bore the sins of the world!
Hail the Holy Spirit who woos us back to God!

Prayer Notes

Prayer Notes

Prayer Notes

Prayer Notes